You should keep trying!
You can ask for help if you need it.

Why?

Because when you finish it, you will feel proud!
And next time it won't be as hard to do.

What should you do if you want
to learn something new?

You are growing up and
learning new things every day!

Sometimes you might be afraid to try something new,
like going down the big slide at the park.
It might be scary at first,
but you should give it a try.
Next time, you won't be as afraid!

Sometimes you might get frustrated
when you are doing something that is hard,
like tying your shoes.
It might be hard at first,
but you should keep trying.
With practice, it will get easier!

You can learn to do new things.
Keep trying when something is hard.
Do more things all by yourself.
This will make you feel proud!

What should you do when you are
doing something that is hard?

You should try it!

Why?

Because learning something new feels good.
Even though you might not be able
to do it very well at first, with practice,
you will get better and better at it.

What should you do if you are
afraid to try something new?

You should think to yourself,
"I can do it!" and then give it a try.

Why?

Because even though it may feel a little scary at first,
you might find out that you really like it!

What should you do when you mess up
something that you are working on?

You should say to yourself, "Oops! I messed up.
Oh well, I'll take my time and try again."

Why?

Because everybody messes up and it is okay!
You just have to keep trying!

What should you do if you know how
to do something all by yourself?